GERM INVADERS
ATTACKING GERMS
WITH SCIENCE

ELSIE OLSON

Big Buddy Books

An Imprint of Abdo Publishing
abdobooks.com

abdobooks.com

Published by Abdo Publishing, a division of ABDO, PO Box 398166, Minneapolis, Minnesota 55439. Copyright © 2021 by Abdo Consulting Group, Inc. International copyrights reserved in all countries. No part of this book may be reproduced in any form without written permission from the publisher. Big Buddy Books™ is a trademark and logo of Abdo Publishing.

Printed in the United States of America, North Mankato, Minnesota
102020
012021

Design: Sarah DeYoung, Mighty Media, Inc.
Production: Mighty Media, Inc.
Editor: Rebecca Felix

Cover Photographs: Shutterstock (all)
Interior Photographs: Shutterstock, pp. 4–7, 9–11, 13, 15, 17–19, 21–23, 25–27, 29; Smithsonian Institution/Flickr, p. 23; Wellcome Collection Gallery/Wikimedia, pp. 12, 26
Design Elements: Shutterstock (all)

Library of Congress Control Number: 2020940277

Publisher's Cataloging-in-Publication Data
Names: Olson, Elsie, author.
Title: Attacking germs with science / by Elsie Olson
Description: Minneapolis, Minnesota : Abdo Publishing, 2021 | Series: Germ invaders | Includes online resources and index
Identifiers: ISBN 9781532194207 (lib. bdg.) | ISBN 9781098213565 (ebook)
Subjects: LCSH: Immunology--Juvenile literature. | Health behavior--Juvenile literature. | Hygiene--Juvenile literature. | Science--Experiments--Juvenile literature. | Viruses--Juvenile literature. | Medicine, Preventive--Juvenile literature.
Classification: DDC 616.079--dc23

CONTENTS

Your Amazing Body 4
When Germs Attack 6
Infections 101 8
Vaccines 10
Viral Infections 14
Bacterial Infections 18
Fungal Infections 22
Protozoan Infections 24
Clean Science 26
Healthy Habits 28
Glossary 30
Online Resources 31
Index 32

YOUR AMAZING BODY

You are amazing! So is your body. Most of the time your body works just fine. But sometimes germs **invade** it. Germs can make you sick. Fortunately, scientists work hard to create cures and treatments.

GET TO KNOW GERMS

Germs are tiny **organisms**. They can live inside people, plants, and animals. There are four main types of germs.

VIRUSES

Viruses are parasitic. This means they cannot survive on their own. They require a host cell to reproduce.

BACTERIA

Bacteria are single-celled creatures. They can survive on their own or inside another living organism.

PROTOZOA

Protozoa are single-celled creatures. Some can survive on their own. Others are parasitic.

FUNGI

Fungi are plant-like organisms. They get their food from people, plants, and animals.

WHEN GERMS ATTACK

Your body is **exposed** to thousands of germs every day. Many don't cause trouble. But some germs **infect** you. Tens of millions of people get infections every year. Germs are spread in many ways.

FROM ANOTHER PERSON

A sick person coughs, sneezes, or talks near you. Their germs enter the air. You breathe in the germ. It attaches to cells inside your body.

FROM FOOD OR WATER

You eat rotten food or drink dirty water, both of which can have germs. These germs can include salmonella and some types of *E. coli*.

FROM A SURFACE

Some viruses and bacteria survive for a short time on a surface. And fungi are found on many bathroom and kitchen surfaces. If you touch germy surfaces and then your eyes, nose, or mouth, the germs can enter your body.

FROM AN INSECT BITE

Insects carrying **diseases** can pass the germs to you if they bite you. Malaria and Lyme disease are spread by insects.

FROM AN INFECTED ANIMAL

Zoonotic diseases can occur when an animal carrying a germ bites a person. They can also occur if a person eats or comes in contact with these animals. Zoonotic diseases include rabies and salmonella.

INFECTIONS 101

Infection occurs when a germ **invades** your body. The germ reproduces. This can harm your cells and cause **toxins** to be set free.

Infections have many **symptoms**. Fever, coughing, and sneezing are some. Others are tiredness or body aches.

Your immune system fights infections. Your body makes antibodies. White blood cells attack the germs. But sometimes your immune system needs help. That's where science comes in!

VACCINES

Vaccines are matter given by shots to help prevent illnesses caused by some viruses and bacteria. These harmful germs are called pathogens. Pathogens with available vaccines include influenza and chicken pox.

Pathogens give off molecules called **antigens**. Vaccines contain antigens. When you receive vaccination, these antigens are put into your body.

Antigens from vaccines won't make you sick. But they trick your immune system into thinking you are. It starts making antibodies.

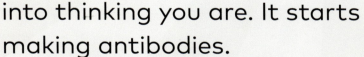

New babies cannot receive some vaccines. Neither can people with weak immune systems. That's why it is important for everyone who can to get vaccinated. There will be fewer people spreading diseases!

Antibodies are special **proteins**. They kill **antigens**. Each antibody is made to attack a specific type of antigen.

Your body stores antibodies. Now if the real pathogen strikes, your immune system is ready. It can attack the germ with the antibodies it has ready. This kills the germs before they can cause an **infection**.

SCIENCE BREAKTHROUGH

Edward Jenner was an English doctor. In 1796, he made germ history. He used pathogens from the milder **disease** cowpox to prevent the deadly smallpox disease. Jenner called his method vaccination.

Edward Jenner

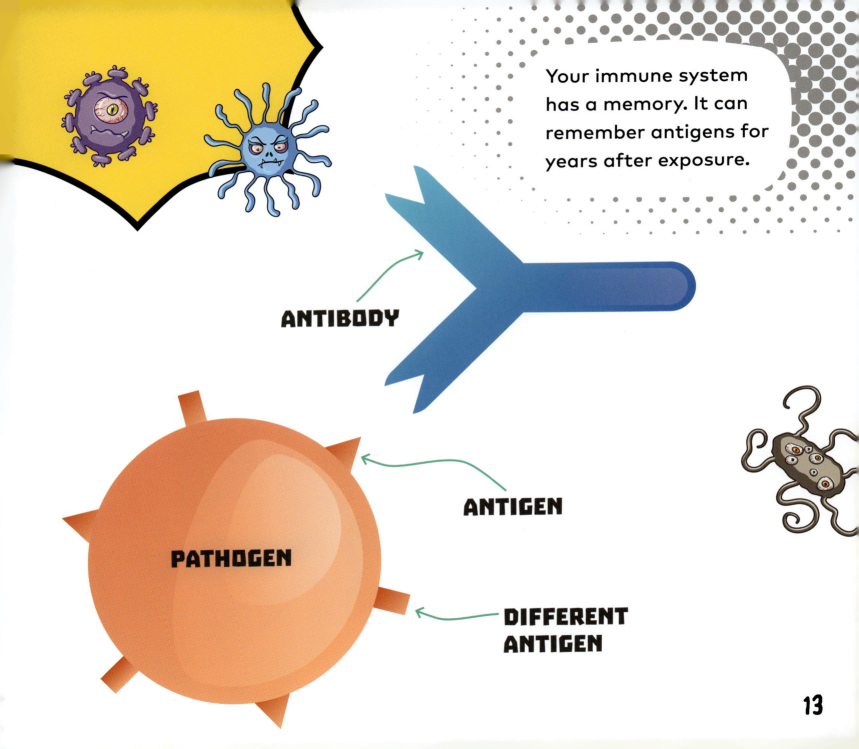

VIRAL INFECTIONS

Some viruses **mutate** often. Different types of a virus are called strains. **Antigens** must match a strain for a vaccine to work well, or for it to even work at all.

Influenza mutates often. Each year, scientists try to make an educated guess about what flu strains will be present. They create a vaccine based on this guess.

But some viruses have more than 100 strains! The common cold is one example. It has too many strains to create vaccines for.

It is important to get a new flu vaccination each year.

Vaccines don't always prevent **infection**. So, then your immune system gets to work! It can take weeks for it to **detect** and destroy a virus. Antiviral medicines can help.

Antivirals bind to a virus **enzyme**. This stops the virus from making copies. Used correctly, antivirals can shorten the amount of time you are sick.

Antivirals are often used to treat the flu.

BACTERIAL INFECTIONS

Bacterial **infections** are most often treated with antibiotics. These medicines have matter that kills bacteria. Some antibiotics attack the bacteria's cell wall. Others prevent the bacteria from reproducing.

Doctors **prescribe** antibiotics for many infections. These include strep throat, food poisoning, and some ear infections.

SCIENCE BREAKTHROUGH

Alexander Fleming was a Scottish doctor. In 1928, he noticed mold on some bacteria he was growing. Anywhere the mold grew, the bacteria didn't. A substance in the mold killed the bacteria! Fleming named the substance penicillin. It is still a common antibiotic.

Alexander Fleming

Strep throat symptoms include feeling very tired. This bacterial infection spreads easily in crowded places, such as on buses or at schools.

Antibiotics can help fight illnesses. But too many can cause problems. If you take antibiotics too often, bacteria inside your body can become resistant to them. This creates super germs. Super germs are very hard to kill.

Antibiotics can also harm good bacteria. These include bacteria that help your **digestive system** work.

For these reasons, it's important to take antibiotics only if, and for as long as, your doctor tells you to.

FUNGAL INFECTIONS

Fungi are all around us. Some can cause rashes or throat **infections**. Other fungal infections are deadly. Meningitis is one. It is a brain or spinal cord infection sometimes caused by fungi.

Fortunately, antifungal drugs were invented in the mid-1900s. They kill fungus or stop it from reproducing.

Nystatin treats human fungal infections. It also treats a fungal infection that kills elm trees!

American scientists Elizabeth Lee Hazen (*left*) and Rachel Fuller Brown (*right*) developed nystatin in 1950. This was one of the first antifungal drugs.

PROTOZOAN INFECTIONS

Protozoa are common all over the world. Some can cause deadly **diseases**. Malaria is one such disease. Its protozoan **parasite** is spread through mosquito bites. Malaria is most common in tropical areas.

Scientists are working on a malaria vaccine. But they have developed other drugs to prevent and cure malaria. Some antimalarial drugs are taken before **exposure**. These drugs help prevent the disease. They kill the parasite larvae before they can spread.

CLEAN SCIENCE

Antonie van Leeuwenhoek was a Dutch scientist. In 1676, he discovered that vinegar killed bacteria. This began **disinfectant** science. Since then, scientists have discovered many chemicals that can kill germs on surfaces.

Disinfectants can be effective. But many are harmful to the body. Never **ingest** disinfectants. And don't touch them without adult guidance.

SCIENCE BREAKTHROUGH

Joseph Lister was a British surgeon in the 1800s. Then, many patients got **infections** after **surgery**. Lister believed this was because doctors rarely washed their hands or tools. He pushed for better doctor and tool cleanliness. As a result, infections decreased!

Joseph Lister

Workers use disinfectants to clean surfaces at hospitals.

HEALTHY HABITS

Scientists have created many ways to fight germs. But these habits can help keep you healthy too!

- ☐ Keep a safe distance from sick people.
- ☐ Don't share dishes with people who are sick.
- ☐ Wash your hands often for at least 20 seconds with soap and water.
- ☐ Avoid touching your face.
- ☐ Cough and sneeze into tissues or your elbow.
- ☐ If you do get sick, stay home and rest! Wear a face mask if you must go out in public.

Infections can be harmful. But thanks to your amazing immune system, science, and some healthy habits, your body is ready to face these germ **invaders**!

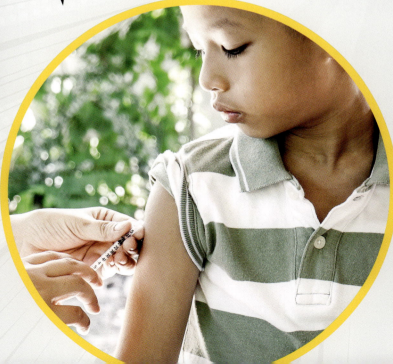

29

GLOSSARY

antigen—a substance that is foreign to the body and causes an immune system response.

detect—to discover or notice.

digestive system (deye-JEHST-iv SIH-stem)—the group of organs that break down food into simpler substances the body can absorb.

disease—a sickness.

disinfectant—a chemical that destroys harmful microorganisms, such as bacteria and fungi, on inanimate surfaces or objects.

enzyme (EHN-zime)—something made in living cells of plants and animals. It helps break down food.

expose—to submit or make accessible to a harmful condition. This experience is called exposure.

infect—to enter and cause disease in. This condition is called an infection.

ingest—to take into the body for digestion.

invade—to enter and spread with the intent to take over. Something that does this is an invader.

mutate—to suddenly change, relating to the genes of a human, a plant, or an animal.

organism—a living thing.

parasite—a living thing that lives in or on another living thing. It gains from its host, which it usually hurts.

prescribe—to order the use of as medicine or treatment.

protein (PROH-teen)—a combination of certain kinds of chemical elements found in all plant and animal cells.

surgery—the treating of sickness or injury by cutting into and repairing body parts.

symptom—a noticeable change in the normal working of the body. A symptom indicates or accompanies disease, sickness, or other malfunction.

toxin—a harmful substance.

ONLINE RESOURCES

To learn more about attacking germs with science, please visit **abdobooklinks.com** or scan this QR code. These links are routinely monitored and updated to provide the most current information available.

INDEX

animals, 5, 7, 24
antibiotics, 18, 20, 21
antibodies, 10, 12
antifungal drugs, 22, 23
antigens, 10, 11, 12, 14
antimalarial drugs, 24
antivirals, 16, 17

bacteria, 5, 6, 7, 10, 11, 18, 19, 20, 26
body aches, 8
breathing, 6

chicken pox, 10
colds, 14
coughing, 6, 8, 28
cowpox, 12

digestive system, 20
disinfectants, 26, 27
doctors, 12, 18, 20, 26

E. coli, 6
ear infections, 18
elm trees, 22
enzymes, 16

face masks, 28
fever, 8, 9

Fleming, Alexander, 18
food poisoning, 18
Fuller, Rachel, 23
fungi, 5, 7, 22, 23

germs spreading, 6, 7, 13, 19, 24
Great Britain, 12, 26

Hazen, Elizabeth Lee, 23

immune system, 8, 10, 11, 12, 13, 16, 28
influenza, 10, 14, 15, 17

Jenner, Edward, 12

Lister, Joseph, 26
Lyme disease, 7

malaria, 7, 24, 25
meningitis, 22
mold, 18
mosquitoes, 24, 25

Netherlands, 26
nystatin, 22, 23

parasites, 5, 24
pathogens, 10, 11, 12

penicillin, 18
plants, 5
protozoa, 5, 24

rabies, 7

salmonella, 6, 7
scientists, 4, 14, 23, 24, 26, 28
Scotland, 18
smallpox, 12
sneezing, 6, 8, 28
strep throat, 18, 19
super germs, 20
symptoms, 6, 8, 9, 19, 28

tiredness, 8, 19
toxins, 8

vaccines, 10, 12, 13, 14, 15, 16, 24
Van Leeuwenhoek, Antonie, 26
viruses, 5, 6, 7, 10, 14, 16

washing hands, 26, 28
white blood cells, 8

zoonotic diseases, 7